NIAGARA FALLS

Victor Bumbalo

BROADWAY PLAY PUBLISHING INC
224 E 62nd St, NY NY 10065-8201
212 772-8334 fax: 212 772-8358
BroadwayPlayPub.com

I0139751

CONTENTS

ABOUT THE AUTHOR

Victor Bumbalo is an award-winning playwright whose plays have been produced world wide. He is the recipient of an Ingram Merrill Award for playwriting. Bumbalo was a finalist for the 2007 Lambda Literary Award for his play QUESTA. NIAGARA FALLS followed its Off-Broadway run with subsequent openings in over fifty cities throughout the United States, England, and Australia. ADAM AND THE EXPERTS opened to critical success Off-Broadway and has had numerous productions in the United States and Canada. WHAT ARE TUESDAYS LIKE? was featured at the Carnegie Mellon Showcase of New Plays at the Contemporary American Theater Festival. Besides playing throughout the United States, WHAT ARE TUESDAYS LIKE? has had productions in Germany, Japan, England, and Sweden. QUESTA premiered in Los Angeles starring Wendie Malick, Dan Lauria, and Dorian Harewood.

A number of Bumbalo's plays are published, including QUESTA and ADAM AND THE EXPERTS by Broadway Play Publishing Inc. TELL appears in an anthology *Gay and Lesbian Plays Today*, published by Heinemann Educational Books Inc, and SHOW is included in *The Best American Short Plays 1992-1993*, published by Applause Theater Book Publishers. WHAT ARE TUESDAYS LIKE? appears in *The Actor's Book of Gay and Lesbian Plays* published by Penguin Books.

Bumbalo has written for several popular television series: *N Y P D Blue, American Gothic, Relativity,* and H B O's *Spawn.* He has also written movies of the week and co-authored a screenplay with Dan Lauria, *The Book of Joe.* He recently wrote a treatment for 20th Century Fox Animation, along with a partner, Ray Shenusay. They have also completed three screenplays, *Dan Decker vs the Zeebians, Road Crew,* and *Crime Pests.*

Bumbalo is the founder and president of the Robert Chesley Foundation.

The author wants to thank the following people for their inspiration, talent, and practical help: Barry Laine, Dan Lauria, John Glines, J Kevin Hanlon, Allan Estes, Judy Engles, Eric Martinsen, George Whitmore, August Ginnochio, James Ross Smith, Michael Powers, Candida Scott Piel, Larry Mitchell, William Casteman, Stephen Greco, David Stuart, and Billy Blackwell.

for Tom

AMERICAN COFFEE

CHARACTERS & SETTING

Connie Poletti
Johnny Poletti

Place: Utica, New York.

Time: Early morning. June 1971

(*Seated at a kitchen table is* CONNIE POLETTI, *a middle-aged housewife. A lighting fixture hangs over the table, illuminating it and the immediate surrounding area. The rest of the stage is dark.*)

(CONNIE, *in her bathrobe, is clutching a cup of coffee. After a few moments,* JOHNNY POLETTI *steps out of the darkness and joins his wife at the table.*)

(*It is five in the morning.*)

(*They attempt to speak in hushed tones so as not to awaken the other people in the house. In highly animated moments the time of day is totally forgotten. Both* CONNIE *and* JOHNNY *are continually adjusting their volume.*)

JOHNNY: Couldn't sleep either, huh?

CONNIE: (*With great difficulty*) Johnny...

JOHNNY: I don't want to see you cry now. Do you hear me? You can cry this afternoon or tonight, but not now.

CONNIE: Johnny...

JOHNNY: Get me a cup of coffee.

(CONNIE *puts her cup down, steps away from the table, and disappears into the darkness.*)

JOHNNY: (*Proudly*) I bet I cry tonight. I bet I break down and cry. And you know something? I bet I don't do it in private. I bet I do it in front of a lot of people. I bet I bawl my eyes out tonight in front of everybody.

(CONNIE *returns to the table with a cup of coffee for her husband and a sugar bowl.*)

JOHNNY: What the hell's with the sugar? You trying to kill me or something? It's been five years since I've put sugar in my coffee.

CONNIE: I'm sorry, Johnny. I wasn't thinking.

JOHNNY: I know, honey. You're thinking about our little bride. Our baby... Our only girl. And how today she's gonna walk down the aisle of Saint Rosalie's and desert us.

(CONNIE *is about to burst into tears.*)

JOHNNY: Not now, Connie. Not now. Tonight, when Sonny Lano and the Half Notes start playing *The Anniversary Waltz*, that's when we'll cry. We'll get up from the banquet table, lead the bridal party and all the family in the dance, and then, right there, right there on the dance floor—maybe they'll even have a spotlight on us—we'll break down. While all our friends are applauding. It'll be so nice,

CONNIE: *(Suddenly)* He's here!

JOHNNY: *(Frightened)* Who?

CONNIE: Him.

JOHNNY: *(Not wanting to believe it)* No.

CONNIE: *(Breaking down)* He's asleep in his room.

JOHNNY: Oh my God!!!

CONNIE: It's not my fault. I swear it's not my fault.

JOHNNY: *(Trying not to explode)* When'd he get in?

CONNIE: Two, three hours ago. I was having this nightmare. We were all at Ma's and I made lasagne and everybody was hollering at me. My mother kept screaming, "The sauce—it's bitter. It's bitter, Connie." And then my sister Rose yells, "Ma, of course it's bitter. She burnt the meat. She always burns the meat." Then I got so nervous that I dropped my plate of lasagne all

over Ma's dining room floor, and it made such a noise.
Only, it wasn't the noise of my plate on Ma's floor.
It was the noise of a taxi door slamming. A real one.
Outside on the street. In front of the house. I looked
outside to see who it could be, and there he was...
our son.

JOHNNY: You knew he was coming, didn't you?
You knew it! You knew he was gonna come and
ruin my whole goddamn day!

CONNIE: (*Trying to calm her husband down*) I swear
to God I didn't know. You heard me on the phone
with him last month. I told him. "Come at Christmas.
Don't bother coming all this way for one day. Your
sister doesn't expect it of you." You heard me tell him.
"Just send her your love and an expensive gift." He
didn't even answer the invitation. Who knew he liked
surprises.

JOHNNY: You sent him an invitation?!!?

CONNIE: Of course I did. I had to. He's our son.

JOHNNY: (*Sarcastically*) No wonder everybody calls you
Connie the Good, Connie the Saint. You always have
to be so goddamn nicey-nicey. Well, let me tell you
something. They also call you Connie the Goof. Even
your own family. Everybody loves telling stories about
the stupid things you do. Like sending an invitation
to a wedding to somebody you don't want to come.
Did you send any of the Mancuso family an invitation?
Of course not. You knew when your father was alive
there was talk that he "kept company" with old lady
Mancuso. So any Mancuso at the wedding would upset
your mother. So even though we still buy our sausage
from them, we won't be seeing any of their faces today,
right? Because none of them got an invitation.
Sometimes, Connie...you can be such a goof.

CONNIE: But we're talking about our son.

JOHNNY: Did you want him at the wedding?

(They stare at each other for a second and then sip their coffee in silence. A few moments pass.)

JOHNNY: How'd he get here.

CONNIE: *(Preoccupied)* He took a taxi.

JOHNNY: *(Sarcastically)* From Los Angeles?

CONNIE: From the airport.

JOHNNY: *(Sipping his coffee)* How's he looking?

CONNIE: Oh, he looks good. All suntanned and handsome. And he's not so skinny any more.

JOHNNY: I swear to God, if he opens his mouth and talks about IT, or if he let's IT slip out in any way, I'll kill him. And then, I'll have to kill myself.

CONNIE: Oh, Johnny don't...don't talk like that. Not on your daughter's wedding day.

JOHNNY: Don't worry. I'm not going to ruin my baby's day. Not me. When he walks in here, I'm going to smile, say hello, and punch him in the arm like I used to. You won't hear one word about IT out of my mouth. Not one word. But I'm warning you, I better not hear him mention IT or I swear I'll....

CONNIE: *(Suddenly)* He's not alone.

JOHNNY: Oh no.

CONNIE: I'm sorry.

JOHNNY: *(Getting hysterical)* Oh no... Oh no....

CONNIE: They're both upstairs. In his room.

JOHNNY: I don't believe you. I'm his father. We used to be pals. He wouldn't do this to me. For Chrissake, tell me it's not true.

CONNIE: It's true.

JOHNNY: Oh my God, Connie, the son of a bitch!
He brought his fairy home!

CONNIE: Sssh. They'll hear you.

JOHNNY: So what?!?

CONNIE: *(Trying to reason with her husband)* Do you want
to wake up Jackie? If she gets up now, she'll get those
puffy circles under her eyes. The ones she gets when
she's tired. And then it'll be your fault if she looks
awful all day long.

JOHNNY: *(Trying to get a hold of himself)* How'd this
happen to me? Tell me how this happened. Haven't
I been a good provider, Connie?

CONNIE: The best, Johnny. The very best.

JOHNNY: Have you, your son or your daughter ever
gone to bed hungry?

CONNIE: Never.

JOHNNY: So I didn't get you a new dress every Easter.
So what? You remember what I used to say about that?

CONNIE: You can't eat a dress.

JOHNNY: That's not what I said. I said fancy clothes
don't collect interest. If you wanted your kids to go to
college, you couldn't be a Mohawk Street fashion plate.
After all, I don't run General Electric. All I do is mop
their lousy floors.

CONNIE: Why didn't you let me help you? I could have
worked. You could have sent me to hairdressing school.

JOHNNY: If I sent you to work, I could never have
looked your father or my own father in the eye.
Now, drop it!

(They sip their coffee in silence for a few seconds.)

CONNIE: *(Begging him)* Please. Please talk to Dominic Fucci.

JOHNNY: He's been dead for ten years.

CONNIE: I know, but maybe you could pray to him or have a Mass said in his name. I'm sure he'd like that.

JOHNNY: I'm warning you, don't start that song and dance again.

CONNIE: All this could be his fault. He may have put the evil eye on us. If only you had let him sing at our wedding. He sang at everybody else's. And he had such a gorgeous voice. So clear and high and loud.

JOHNNY: I didn't want a queer to sing at my wedding.

CONNIE: But you didn't have to say that in front of him. He was so hurt. I can still see his little round face.

JOHNNY: I didn't know he was standing there. It was Sunday. Nicky's was crowded.

CONNIE: I don't understand how you could have missed him. He was standing right next to Father Brandesi at the espresso bar.

JOHNNY: Will you forget it.

CONNIE: I can't help it. I keep thinking that when Dominic died, Our Lord asked him, because he had such a beautiful voice and because he was such a close friend of Father Brandesi, if there was one wish he wanted. And he said to God, "Make one of the Poletti children just like me...."

JOHNNY: *(Getting angry)* That's nuts. You're thinking goofy again, Connie.

CONNIE: "...Make one of the Poletti children just like me."*(Breaking down)* And God did. So we didn't have one at our wedding. Instead, we got one in our family for the rest of our lives.

JOHNNY: Dominic Fucci didn't do this. God doesn't listen to those kind of people.

CONNIE: We don't know that.

JOHNNY: Ask a priest. He'll tell you.

CONNIE: You know, when our son sent us the letter explaining to us what he was and how happy he was about it.... How many years ago was that?

JOHNNY: It'll be five years on May 13th.

CONNIE: I never told you this, but the next day after you went to work, I bought some flowers and went to Dominic's grave. I begged him to take the curse off our son. If only we asked him to sing at our wedding.

JOHNNY: I wanted my cousin Lucille to sing.

CONNIE: Why, Johnny, why? You knew the dear departed soul was a drunk. She was plowed at ten that morning and couldn't remember one word to the *Ave Maria*. She had to hum it.

JOHNNY: Would you shut up about Lucille and Dominic. They have nothing to do with our son. I'll tell you why we got one in our family. We got no luck. You had no luck your entire life. Wait a minute. A few years ago you won fifty dollars at Bingo. That was all the luck you're ever gonna see. And me, for thirty-five years I've been playing the football pool, and I've never hit it once. I'm telling you, Connie, it's embarrassing. Now, you put our two lives together and what do you expect to get? A son who's gonna give you happy Christmases or a powder puff who's gonna break your heart? You're gonna get the powder puff. Luck is like fat or money. You either have a disposition towards it or you don't.

CONNIE: (*Trying to convince her husband and herself*) Maybe we're getting nervous for nothing. Maybe everything will be all right. Maybe nobody at the wedding will put two and two together. The boys look real regular. So maybe nobody will notice.

JOHNNY: Are blind people coming to the wedding? Because they'd be the only ones who wouldn't notice the two men dancing together.

CONNIE: They're not going to dance.

JOHNNY: Of course they are. These kind of people love to dance. I saw it on the news.

CONNIE: Our son never liked to dance.

JOHNNY: That's when he was dancing with girls. Maybe he feels different about it now. Maybe now, he's a regular Ginger Rogers. And today I was gonna hold my head up high. So my daughter didn't get married until she was thirty....

CONNIE: Thirty-one.

JOHNNY: Thirty. Don't age the poor thing so fast.

CONNIE: She's thirty-one. When she turned thirty, we had to send for Doctor Robertello to stop her from crying.

JOHNNY: What the hell difference does it make?

CONNIE: I was correcting you in case somebody asked you how old your daughter was. That's all.

JOHNNY: What do you want me to do? Walk around with a sign that says the bride's thirty-one?

CONNIE: There's nothing wrong with being thirty-one.

JOHNNY: That's what I was trying to say. It's all right to be on the older side and get married if you land something like Vinnie Ventura. Can you imagine, she's hitching up with the biggest furriers in Utica. The Venturas of Park Lane. I can count the times I've been to that ritzy neighborhood. And now, I'll be going there all the time. My own daughter is going to be living in the Venturas' converted garage. What a wedding present they're giving the kids. Turning their garage into a palace. The dough they're soaking into that place.

CONNIE: I only wish Vinnie were better looking.

JOHNNY: I don't. I'm glad he's on the homely side. This way he'll stay home nights.

CONNIE: You don't have to be good-looking to run around. Look at your brother and his women.

JOHNNY: What are you talking about? My brother's handsome. He's a good-looking son of a bitch. You got eyes up your ass? What's he look like?

CONNIE: Who?

JOHNNY: Your son's who.

CONNIE: Oh him. Oooooh, is he good-looking. He's real tall, much taller than our son, and he looks very strong.

JOHNNY: An American?

CONNIE: Yes. Blond, blue eyes, everything. I wish Vinnie were a little good-looking like that.

JOHNNY: Will you shut up about Vinnie. You don't have to go to bed with him. All you have to do is cook him a meal every other Sunday.... Oh Jesus, I hope he takes her on their honeymoon.

CONNIE: He's not going to leave her home.

JOHNNY: He might after he finds out. The Venturas might order their son to leave her. They might not want, excuse the expression... (Whispering) ...a homosexual in the family.

CONNIE: Don't say that!

JOHNNY: They might think that it runs in the blood.
That the Poletti women can't have real sons.

CONNIE: We got a real son.

JOHNNY: Real sons bring their wives and children into
your home. They give one of their kids your first name
so that you can forget, for a few minutes, that you're
getting old and on your way to the grave.

CONNIE: How you used to love that boy. Hours
and hours you used to sit together playing Chinese
Checkers.

JOHNNY: Did you ever hear me say I don't love him.
I love him. He's my son, and I love him. I only hate
who he is. What's he do?

CONNIE: Who?

JOHNNY: The blond bombshell.

CONNIE: I don't know. I forgot.

JOHNNY: You forgot! For five years I've let you call
California twice a month, and you never found out
in all that time what this guy does?

CONNIE: I thought you didn't want to know anything
about them.

JOHNNY: (Sarcastically) Now that they're both sleeping
in my house, I'm more interested. What's he do?

CONNIE: He used to work for the phone company.

JOHNNY: I used to be a paper boy. What's he do now,
Connie?

CONNIE: It has something to do with music. I don't
know.

JOHNNY: Come on, tell me.

CONNIE: I don't know what he does. If you're so
curious, go ask him.

JOHNNY: Swear on your daughter's happiness that you don't know. Come on, swear.

CONNIE: He plays records.

JOHNNY: Plays records?!? Where? In his room, on the radio, in a store...

CONNIE: At dances.

JOHNNY: He plays records at dances, and this is called a job. I like to turn on the T V now and then. Do you think I can get a job doing that?

CONNIE: There must be more to it than putting on a record.

JOHNNY: Well, one thing is for sure. I bet he's a regular Katherine Murray.

CONNIE: I don't think that boy likes to dance. He doesn't look like the dancing type. And if he didn't bring another pair of shoes with him, he couldn't possibly dance in those boots he was wearing.

JOHNNY: He wasn't wearing high heels, was he?

CONNIE: No. I told you. He was very masculine. They were boots. They were big and black. They were big, black boots.

JOHNNY: *(Getting worried)* Oh no. I hope he's not one of those Butches.

CONNIE: What are they?

JOHNNY: They're these real rough homos who love running around in motorcycle jackets. They had a whole chapter on them in this book I was reading called *Spotting the Homosexual.*

CONNIE: I never saw you reading a book like that.

JOHNNY: I read it while you were out of the house. It was a highly intelligent book. A little on the raw side, but good. It was written by a very smart doctor. It described the different varieties of homosexuals. What each kind liked to think about, what each kind liked to eat, what movies they went to, what singers they were crazy about. And it talked a lot about these toughies, and you don't want to hear what those people do.

CONNIE: What do they do?

JOHNNY: It has to do with sex.

CONNIE: I don't want to hear.

JOHNNY: Good girl.

(JOHNNY *raises his cup to show* CONNIE *that it is empty. She immediately gets up from the table, disappears for a moment, and returns with the coffee pot. She refills* JOHNNY's *cup and then disappears again to return the coffee pot to the stove.* JOHNNY *is still holding his cup in midair.* CONNIE *re-emerges out of the darkness with a carton of milk. She adds milk to* JOHNNY's *coffee, stirs it for him, and then takes her place back at the table.* JOHNNY *takes a sip of his coffee.)*

JOHNNY: Remember when your son was living in New York? How every time he came home for a visit, every time, he had the flu? Every Christmas he spent locked in his room sick. That's what I mean by our luck. Where, Connie, where's his flu now?

(CONNIE *makes the sign of the cross.)*

JOHNNY: What are you doing?

CONNIE: I'm asking God not to listen to you.

JOHNNY: Don't worry. He never has. He's not gonna start now.

CONNIE: Don't talk like that. Your life's not miserable. It's hard and boring, and you might not be having a good time, but at least you're getting through it in one piece.

JOHNNY: Those boys can't walk into the Cherry Valley Inn tonight. Go get your sleeping pills.

CONNIE: What? What are you talking about?

JOHNNY: Your sleeping pills. Get them.

CONNIE: I don't have any. I never had any. I'm no drug addict.

JOHNNY: Don't lie, Connie. I told Doctor Robertello to give you some pills so I could sleep nights.

CONNIE: So you could sleep?!?

JOHNNY: Yeah. All your tossing and turning was getting on my nerves. I called Robertello and told him that when you came in for your check-up to give you something that would knock you out. Now, go get those pills.

CONNIE: What are you going to do with them?

JOHNNY: I want to see them.

CONNIE: Why?

JOHNNY: Jesus Christ. *(He gets up and exits into the darkness.)*

CONNIE: *(With a loud whisper after him)* Don't wake up the kids. *(She makes a sign of the cross. Quietly, so her husband does not hear her)* Dear Mother of God, Good Holy Mother, this is Connie Poletti. Grant me one wish, this one favor I'm going to ask you, and I promise I'll stay up all night tomorrow saying the rosary to you. All night, dear sweet gentle Mary. Kneeling. Right here, right here in the kitchen where there'll be no rug under my knees to cushion the pain. Okay? Now, here's what I want. Please, Precious Virgin, don't let anything embarrassing happen today. Let there be just a wedding that's remembered only because the bride looked pretty and the food was exceptionally delicious. Thank you, dear Heavenly Mother. *(She signs off with the*

sign of the cross. She then makes another sign of the cross.)
Dominic? Dominic, you there? *Come sta? Sta bene?* Oh,
excuse me, Dominic, you didn't speak Italian, did you?
I thought you did because you sang in it so beautifully.
Just like a *paesano.* But your mother didn't want you to
learn the language, did she? She wanted you to be a
hundred percent American. And you were. I always
thought you were a one hundred percent American
man. I did. I swear I did. Now listen, if you see to it that
the boys act nice and don't humiliate Mister Poletti—
now listen, Dominic—on All Souls' Day, I'll bring a
dozen roses to your grave. You heard me. One full
dozen. You'd be really impressed with this offer,
Dominic, if you knew the price of roses today.
And maybe I'll put a tag on the bouquet that will say
something like— "With all my love, Karen,"a good
American name. What do you think of that, Dominic?
Won't that start people talking? Won't that confuse
them? Maybe after they see the tag I write, they'll
finally stop calling you names. One dozen roses,
Dominic, to spruce up your grave. All you got to
do is make those boys act normal. You know, like
they go out with girls. No offense, Dominic, no offense.
(She quickly signs off with another sign of the cross.)

*(JOHNNY returns to the kitchen table with the pot of coffee
and a bottle of pills.)*

CONNIE: How'd you know where I kept them?

JOHNNY: A few weeks ago in the middle of the night
I heard you go into your brassiere drawer. I knew you
didn't need a bra at three in the morning.

CONNIE: What are you going to do with them?

JOHNNY: You're going to give them to the boys in their
coffee.

CONNIE: Oh no, oh no! No! Johnny, listen to yourself.
That's insane. We can't do that. We can't poison our
own son.

JOHNNY: *(Breaking the capsules of sleeping pills into the
coffee and trying to act very reasonable.)* We're not
poisoning him. We're just putting him to sleep.

CONNIE: He's not a dog.

JOHNNY: Not permanently. For eight hours. We gave
him his life, didn't we? Well, we can ask him for eight
hours back.

CONNIE: We can't, we can't do this. Not in front of Our
Lord we can't.

JOHNNY: Oh yes we can. He's a man. He'd understand.

CONNIE: Honey, please stop acting like a maniac.
(Trying to reason with him) Look, maybe when they
get up we can all sit down and have a sort of...talk.

JOHNNY: About what? IT? All of us?!? What are you,
a lunatic? What did I tell you five years ago? That as
long as I lived I would never talk about *that* with my
son. I can't talk about *that* kind of thing with *those* kind
of people. What do you want, to give me a heart attack
or something? Jesus, sometimes Connie...

CONNIE: All right, all right! *(Begging him)* But please,
give me a chance to talk with them.

JOHNNY: What would you say?

CONNIE: *(Thinking)* Well...a...first I'd...a...make a big
breakfast. I wonder if our son still likes waffles. Maybe
you should go out and get a pound of bacon for the
American. You know how those people love their
bacon and eggs. Do you think he'd mind if I made
the toast with Italian bread?

JOHNNY: What the hell are you going on about food for?

CONNIE: Because men are always in a better mood after they eat. This I know. So... when they're in their better mood, I'd pour myself a cup of coffee, sit down at the table with them and tell them... *(Proudly, having finally gotten the idea what to say)* ...that a wedding is a sacred and holy thing and that during such a solemn occasion, it would be a sin if they got up and danced.

JOHNNY: You're making the wedding sound like a funeral. They'd laugh in your face if you talked like that.

CONNIE: Then tell me what I should say?

JOHNNY: I'm not saying I'm going to, but if I let you talk to them, I couldn't be here when you did it.

CONNIE: Of course not. I'd send you out for milk or something. And I'd make sure we were finished by the time you got back. Now, what should I say?

JOHNNY: You'd have to be strong with them. You'd have to tell them that you don't want to see them give each other any funny looks or little winks. It would be great if our son made a pass at a woman today. Right in front of everybody. Do you think he'd do something like that for me?

CONNIE: He's not the type. He's always been on the shy side.

JOHNNY: How can we let him come to the reception? He might make a pass at a man.

CONNIE: He's with his friend, and they're kind of...acouple.

JOHNNY: Oh... *(He thinks for a moment.)* They can't come. Who wants to look at them touching each other, holding hands, giving each other little kisses here and there....

CONNIE: They wouldn't do anything like that.

JOHNNY: *(Getting angry)* Of course they would! They're queers!

CONNIE: Sssh!! They might hear you!

JOHNNY: What do you think queers do? They do the same thing everybody else does, only they do it to each other.

CONNIE: *(In an intense whisper)* Keep it down.

JOHNNY: And they're gonna be doing those things right in front of your mother and your sister Rose.

CONNIE: Ma wouldn't know what any of it meant.

JOHNNY: But your sister Rose, with her two perfect daughters and two perfect sons, would be glad to tell her. Can't you hear her? *(Imitating Rose)* "Poor Connie, only one boy, and he's not quite right. I knew she'd turn him into a sissy."

CONNIE: *(Turning on JOHNNY)* You think it's my fault, don't you? You think it's my fault that he's that way.

JOHNNY: I never said that. In these five awful years I never said anything like that. I only said what your sister Rose would say.

CONNIE: And you agree with her.

JOHNNY: Well, to this day, I still can't understand why you didn't buy his Communion suit at Rizzi's.

CONNIE: His Communion suit?!?!?

JOHNNY: Yes, his Communion suit. When he took First Holy Communion, he was the only boy, the only one, who got his Communion suit from Syracuse. You had to go all the way to Syracuse on a bus. Why? Why couldn't you shop at Rizzi's like everybody else?

CONNIE: Rizzi always dressed the boys like little old men.

JOHNNY: That suit stood out. I was so embarrassed.
It was so white. Whiter than anybody else's. And that
material, it was funny. I bet it was dress material.
And what did you do to his hair? Did you set it or
something?

CONNIE: He has naturally curly hair. I knew. I knew
you blamed me. Why is it? Why is it they always blame
the mothers? Well, let me tell you something. I didn't
read the book you read, but I read a book about it too.
And guess who my book blamed? The fathers.

JOHNNY: Your book doesn't know what it's talking
about.

CONNIE: It must know something because I got it in a
library.

JOHNNY: When did you ever go to a library?

CONNIE: I go there sometimes.

JOHNNY: What the hell for?

CONNIE: I like to look at the magazines. *Seventeen, House
Beautiful*, those pretty ones on travel....

JOHNNY: So now you're calling me cheap. Because I
can't afford to keep you in every stupid magazine that
comes out, you've got to announce it to all of Utica.
I don't want you to go there again.

CONNIE: Nobody's ever seen me there, I swear.

JOHNNY: You heard me. I don't want you to go there.
That library stinks.

CONNIE: No, it doesn't!

JOHNNY: That book you got there was bullshit.
I was a good father!

CONNIE: I know you were, Johnny. I know you were.
It's just that my book said that sometimes when the
fathers were absent...

JOHNNY: Absent?!!? Where did I ever go? When did I
ever have one dime to go anyplace? Oh yeah, on Friday
nights I come home an hour late. My buddies and I like
to go out and have a beer together. Who wrote your
book?

CONNIE: I don't know. Some woman.

JOHNNY: And you believed her? My book was written
by a doctor. Now, who's book you gonna believe?
The one written by the doctor, who we know spent
a lot of years in school, or the one written by the
lady who, I betcha, raised a fruit after her rummy
of a husband walked out on her.

CONNIE: You don't know if that's true.

JOHNNY: The lady or the doctor, Connie?

CONNIE: Can I go back to the library?

JOHNNY: The lady or the doctor?

CONNIE: The doctor, I guess.... But I was a good mother.

JOHNNY: And I was a good father.

CONNIE: Wasn't I a good mother?

JOHNNY: You tried.

*(They drink their coffee in silence for a moment as they both
stare at the coffee pot.)*

JOHNNY: This coffee is the only answer.

CONNIE: No!

JOHNNY: *(Trying to make his plan sound reasonable)* Now,
here's what we do. You wake up the boys and tell them
that I'm anxious to see my son before Jackie gets up and
the excitement of the wedding carries us all away.

CONNIE: *(Praying)* Forgive this man, oh Lord, he knows
not what he does.

JOHNNY: *(Threateningly)* Do you want your mother to get a heart attack?

CONNIE: Ooh, don't say that. Don't even think that.

JOHNNY: Your mother's a little on the nervous side lately, on account of them tearing down Saint Anthony's and putting up a Baskin-Robbins, and something like this, especially with your sister Rose giving her all the gory details, can push her right over. I'm not saying it would, but it might. What an awful memory that would be for Jackie. To have her grandmother croak on her wedding day.

CONNIE: *(Worried)* Do you really think Rose would figure things out and tell Ma?

JOHNNY: *(Capitalizing on his wife's fear)* Of course she would. Rose is a smart woman. As soon as the boys walked into Saint Rosalie's Church, her wheels would begin. *(Imitating Rose)* "Who's that boy my nephew's with? Oh yeah, his roommate. He brought his roommate...on a plane...all the way from Los Angeles... to attend his sister's wedding. That's interesting." And with those famous eagle eyes she would study her nephew and the other one until she put it all together. Then all day long, every time she would look at our son, she'd choke up. People would begin asking her, "Rose, why you taking this wedding so hard?" And she would say *(Imitating Rose)* "It's not the wedding. It's something else. Something I can't tell you. Something I can't tell nobody. But I gotta tell somebody. I can't keep it in any more. If I do, it'll drive me crazy. It's my nephew. You see that man, the one standing so close to him...." "And this she'd do again and again, all day and all night, until everybody at the wedding knew—even the help in the kitchen. Until everybody had one thing on their minds—not the bride, not the groom, not the four thousand dollars I shelled out for this affair—but only one thing—queers.

CONNIE: Do you think Jackie would elope?

JOHNNY: It's too late. The reception's already paid for. *(Suddenly)* Ssssh.

CONNIE: What?!?

JOHNNY: I heard something. Somebody's awake. Christ, suppose they're listening to us. Go and see if they're asleep.

CONNIE: I didn't hear anything. It's quiet.

JOHNNY: Go and check on them. Make sure they're asleep. I don't want them to know what we're going to do. They might get mad and plan something really revolting. I don't want them calling their friends and telling them to crash the wedding.

CONNIE: Our son doesn't know anybody in Utica anymore.

JOHNNY: He might be a member of the military gays.

CONNIE: What are they?

JOHNNY: They're the ones that like parades. There are organizations of them now. All over the country. All they'd have to do is make one phone call, and they'd all be outside of the church waiting for us. With signs. They love carrying signs. Go and check on them.

(CONNIE does not move.)

JOHNNY: What are you waiting for?

CONNIE: I'm afraid. Suppose they're...you know?

JOHNNY: What?

CONNIE: Suppose they're doing...you know what?

JOHNNY: It's the middle of the night. They just came from a long trip. They're tired. They're either asleep or they're listening to us. Now, go find out.

CONNIE: But they're men.

JOHNNY: What's that mean?

CONNIE: Men sometimes like to do it in the middle of
the night.

JOHNNY: *(Getting angry)* What are you talking about?

CONNIE: Remember when we visited Cousin Stella in
Niagara Falls? We got lost and had to drive for hours
and hours. You were so exhausted, and I got so worried
that you'd fall asleep at the wheel and kill us on our
way to the only vacation we ever took. It was four
o'clock in the morning before Cousin Stella settled us
in our room. Then you told me you were over-tired,
and we had to do it so you could relax and get to sleep.

JOHNNY: They didn't drive. They took a plane. Now,
go see if they're listening.

CONNIE: I'll put my ears to the door, but I won't peek in
if I hear any noise.

JOHNNY: Would you do what I say?!?

CONNIE: *(Getting up and moving away from the table)*
I just hope they're wearing pajamas.

(After CONNIE *disappears,* JOHNNY *gets up from the table
and also disappears into the darkness. He returns to the table
with two cookies. He starts wolfing them down and being
very cautious about the crumbs. He wants to finish the
cookies before* CONNIE *returns. After a few moments,*
CONNIE *steps back into the light and seats herself at the
table.)*

CONNIE: What are you eating?

JOHNNY: *(With his mouth full, spitting out a few crumbs)*
Nothing.

CONNIE: *(Worried)* You're not supposed to have any
sweets.

JOHNNY: One cookie. One cookie isn't going to kill me.

CONNIE: How was it?

JOHNNY: I don't want to say anything, but they came out too dry. Yours always come out on the dry side. You should have let my mother make them.

CONNIE: Your mother did make them.

JOHNNY: You're lying.

CONNIE: I always put the lemon peel in mine, your mother puts the orange. What did you taste? The lemon or the orange?

JOHNNY: Oh Jesus, I hope she's not losing her touch. Are they asleep?

CONNIE: Yes. Sound asleep. You know your son, he snores just like you.

JOHNNY: And his friend, he's in bed with him?

CONNIE: (Sarcastically) No, he's sleeping on a shelf.

JOHNNY: (Pushing the coffee pot in CONNIE's direction) Now, heat the coffee and then go wake them up.

CONNIE: No! (She grabs the coffee pot and clutches it in her lap.)

JOHNNY: Look, I don't want old man Williams making fun of me. For twenty-five years I've had to work under that bastard, and I'm not giving him another reason to look down on me. If there was any justice in the world, Connie, God would have made the rich have all the fairy sons. This way when we poor people have to look up to them and kiss their lily-white asses we could at least get in a few good laughs.

CONNIE: The rich got them too. My book said they come in all families.

JOHNNY: I don't want the guys in my plant writing dirty things about my son on the bathroom walls.

CONNIE: Grown men write on bathroom walls?

JOHNNY: They sure do, and I'm the jerk who's paid to clean it up. Now, gimme the pot.

CONNIE: Never!!!

JOHNNY: Honey, you're taking this much too serious. What we're gonna do is best for everybody. We'll knock those boys out before Jackie gets up. Then when our bride wakes up, we'll tell her we got some good news for her and some bad news.

CONNIE: What are you going to say? The good news is: it's not raining, and the bad news is: your mother's in the bathroom slitting her throat.

JOHNNY: Don't be such a dope. It's just a few pills in a cup of coffee. We'll tell her, her brother's here, with his friend, and they're both in bed with the flu.

CONNIE: She'll want to say hello.

JOHNNY: Not if we tell her this flu is very catchy. She's waited too long to go on this honeymoon. Now, get moving!

CONNIE: *(Clutching the pot even more firmly)* This pot's going no place.

JOHNNY: Okay. You asked for it. Now, you open your ears and listen loud and clear. You either do as I say or you don't. Your marriage vows either mean something to you or they don't.

CONNIE: What do you mean?

JOHNNY: Love, honor, and *obey*, Connie. *Obey*, Connie.

CONNIE: They don't say that any more.

JOHNNY: I don't care what they say now. That's what they said when your father gave you to me. Now, are you going to put that pot on the stove or am I going to have to have a serious talk with the boys? What's it going to be?

CONNIE: What do you mean a serious talk?

JOHNNY: Mention IT. Talk about IT. Tell them what I think about IT. Tell them that I don't want two people with IT at the wedding. And then, you know what will happen, don't you? Because gay boy or not, he's got the Poletti temper. He's going to get pissed, tell us to go to hell, walk out that door, and we'll never lay eyes on him again. And who's fault will this be? Not mine. No, siree. Because if he sleeps through the wedding, there is no reason, as long as he keeps his mouth shut, for me ever to mention IT. I'll be able to be his father; he'll be able to be my son. And when you call him in California, I might even get on the phone and say hello. But if he walks out of this house and changes his phone number out there, and we never see him again, never till our dying day, well, who's fault is it going to be? Come on, tell me?

(CONNIE *slowly places the coffee pot back on the table.*)

JOHNNY: Good girl. To show you I'm not such an S-O-B, after the wedding, I'll take the boys out for a treat. Maybe even to Rizzi's. I'll buy them a couple of suits.

CONNIE: The Lord knew that someday we were going to do something like this. That's why he gave us only two children. And all these years we believed the doctors when they told us your (*Lowering her voice*) "juice" wasn't strong enough for me.

JOHNNY: Shut up, will you? You promised never to talk about that.

CONNIE: You shouldn't feel bad any more. It wasn't your fault. It was the Lord's. He was protecting children from us.

JOHNNY: It's getting late. You better wake them up.

CONNIE: How are we going to sleep nights?

JOHNNY: Don't worry. If we have any trouble, Doctor Robertello will give us something.

CONNIE: What if they drink tea?

JOHNNY: We'll put a couple of pills in their tea.

CONNIE: What if they drink and eat nothing for breakfast. One of my magazines told me that those people in California love to fast.

JOHNNY: I'll put the pills in their toothpaste if I have to.

CONNIE: I feel like the entire Holy Family is watching us. Mary, she's crying now, teeny tears made out of blood. And she's asking her son, "Is this what mothers have come to?"

JOHNNY: She shouldn't be on such a high horse. Her son was all right.

CONNIE: Yeah, but he didn't go out with girls either.

JOHNNY: Oh for God's sake, will you stop stalling.

CONNIE: And Joseph, he's getting ready to spit on you. Johnny, we can't afford getting on the Holy Family's "poop" list.

JOHNNY: Move your ass!

CONNIE: Please let the boys come to the wedding. If you do, I swear every Sunday you'll be eating manicotti. That's right. Every Saturday night I'll have to stay home so I can stuff those noodles for you. And every Friday, guess what you're gonna be having? *Zuppa di pesce.* And you know how I can't stand the smell of fish.

JOHNNY: If you don't get going and do what I say, your son isn't the only thing you'll never be seeing again. I promise you...are you listening? I swear, I will never... are you hearing me? ...Never let you go to Bingo again.

CONNIE: What?!!?

JOHNNY: That's right. You'll never walk into the basement of Saint Rosalie's Church or the Knights of Columbus Hall again. You're not gonna hear anybody say your favorite words, "under B-13," ever again. You're gonna have to stay home with me every Tuesday and Sunday night.

CONNIE: *(Begging)* Bingo's my only pleasure. Please, it's only two hours each night. That's just four hours a week. I'm home all the rest of the time. And it's the only time I get to see my girlfriend.

JOHNNY: You call that nut a girlfriend?

CONNIE: I know nobody likes poor Rita. Everybody says she's a crazy old maid who talks too loud. It's not her mind that's gone bad, Johnny. It's her ears. She's deaf. That's why she talks funny.

JOHNNY: Well, you won't be seeing her at Bingo any more.

CONNIE: *(Beginning to break down)* I'm her only friend. She looks forward to seeing me. And, Johnny, I love the game. It excites me.

JOHNNY: Even your own family is making fun of you. It's embarrassing. I'm telling you you're showing your lack of education. Only somebody who never went to high school could get a thrill putting popcorn kernels on a bingo card.

CONNIE: A lot you know, we use magic markers now.

JOHNNY: I don't care if you use M & Ms. My hard-earned cash isn't buying you another Bingo card.

CONNIE: Then I'll steal the money. I'll stand in front
of the library with a tin cup and beg for it.

JOHNNY: Don't act stupid.

CONNIE: I know. I'm too dumb. Rita's too nuts.
Our boy's too queer. What are you? The only
perfect creature God ever made? No more Bingo!
You lousy...penny pinching...

JOHNNY: Watch it, Connie! Watch your mouth!

CONNIE: How dare you deny me my Bingo?!?

JOHNNY: I wasn't born yesterday. I'm not throwing out
another dime on a disobedient wife. I'm no fool.

CONNIE: *(Furious)* Three dollars each time I go to Bingo.
That's all I cost you. Oh no, I'm sorry. I'm lying to you.
It's five dollars each time. I go. That's right. I'm costing
you ten dollars a week. That's four more dollars than
you knew about. Can you guess where I get it? I steal it.
From our food money. Four dollars a week I take out of
our stomachs. Now, guess what I do with it? I treat that
"lunatic" Rita to coffee. And sometimes she orders a
piece of pie. Blueberry to be precise. I buy that for her
too. Oh, once in a while the pie costs me forty-five cents
more because she likes a little whipped cream with it.
You know why I do it? It makes me happy. I love
treating poor Rita to coffee. It makes both of us feel
special. And I'm going to continue doing it. And I don't
care if I have to steal the money from Saint Rosalie's
collection box.

JOHNNY: If your father could hear you now, he'd turn
over in his grave.

CONNIE: Let him!

JOHNNY: Connie!

CONNIE: And let all the fathers of all the dumb Connies
turn over with him.

JOHNNY: *(Making the sign of the cross)* Dear Jesus, don't listen to her. It's her mind. It snapped.

CONNIE: Don't apologize to Our Lord for me. He knows what I mean. He knows my father. All I remember about him is the back of his hand and the toast he made the day of our wedding. Do you remember it? *(Imitating her father)* "My daughter, she's not very smart, she's a little bit clumsy, but she'll keep a good house." He didn't even say what a pretty bride I made.

JOHNNY: Lower your voice. You're gonna wake up the whole house.

CONNIE: Good! It's time everybody got up. We've got a wedding to go to.

JOHNNY: Those boys aren't coming.

CONNIE: I think they are.

JOHNNY: You're not ruining today. You're not ruining *my* wedding.

CONNIE: It's *my* wedding too.

JOHNNY: Did you write out all the checks?

CONNIE: Did you give birth to the bride?

JOHNNY: If he's there, with all the mouths going, nobody's gonna hear the ceremony.

CONNIE: If everybody wants to be concerned with what my son does with that thing between his legs, that's their business. I myself am not so interested any more.

JOHNNY: Oh my God, you're beginning to talk like a trollop.

CONNIE: No more Bingo! After thirty-two years of cooking, cleaning, and Sunday afternoon football.

JOHNNY: Rant. Rant all you want. But he can't come. Don't you give a shit what people are gonna say?

CONNIE: Why should I? You told me they already call
me The Goof.

JOHNNY: I told all the guys in my shop that my son was
some big L A stud.

CONNIE: *(Sarcastically)* He could be. Maybe he cheats
on his friend. Maybe he's a regular man's man.
A heartbreaker. The love-them-and-leave-them type.
Would that make you feel any happier?

JOHNNY: What a wife! What a wife I'm saddled with!

CONNIE: Do people pity you, Johnny? What do they
say? That I don't have Rose's hotshot figure? That you
can't eat off my floors? That my sauce isn't as good as
your mother's? But how could it be? We all know that
your mother got her recipe from God. She makes the
same sauce they serve in heaven.

JOHNNY: All right, keep ranting. But let me tell you,
either he sleeps through the day or I finally talk to him.

CONNIE: Once he's up, he's not going back to bed. And
after twenty-seven years of us never talking to that boy,
we're not starting today.

JOHNNY: Who the hell do you think you are?

CONNIE: I'm a Bingo fanatic with a loony-tune for a
girlfriend. I'm also the mother of two children. I have
a *thirty-one-year-old* daughter who the other day said,
"Ma, you know, you're a nice woman." Just like that,
she called her own mother a nice woman. She likes and
respects me. She thinks I'm talented. I overheard her
telling her girlfriend, Maggie, the big redhead with the
mole, that I, without one decent dress in my closet, can
put together a good outfit. And I have a son who thinks
it's important that I smile once in a while. Ever since he
was a little kid, any time he thinks I'm upset about
something, he has to tell me a few jokes. Tonight the
poor boy told me three before he went to bed. Two of

them I didn't even understand. He doesn't think I'm such a dope. I want to be with those two people today, and the people that they love. Everybody else can go take a flying shit.

JOHNNY: If you keep talking like this, I'm gonna have to have you locked up.

CONNIE: Tomorrow you can try to do whatever you want to me. Today, you're following my orders.

JOHNNY: What the hell makes you think so?

CONNIE: 'Cause you don't like scenes. You don't like anything out of the ordinary. And if you don't do what I say, I'm going to make such a commotion at this wedding that they'll be talking about it long after we die and have to go meet Dominic. I won't do it while Jackie's around. I'll wait until she leaves the reception hall to go on her honeymoon. Then I'm gonna go up on the stage with the band, grab the microphone, and I'm gonna give a speech. I'll tell everybody about our marriage, and why it is I gotta leave you. I'll tell them how on the holidays you water down the booze. How you're always crying poor house, yet you got a secret bank account with twelve hundred and forty-six dollars in it.

JOHNNY: I told you never to go near my tackle box.

CONNIE: The kid next door wanted to borrow a fishhook. Who knew it was a treasure chest. And then I'll tell everybody about our son, his letter, and how you treated the boy after that. And with the microphone still in my hand, I'll get down on my knees, call out to Our Lord, and beg his forgiveness for treating my only son like you told me I had to.

JOHNNY: You wouldn't dare....

CONNIE: So when you bring everybody home for a few drinks, I'll be the entertainment. You can all watch me pack.

JOHNNY: You wouldn't dare act like an imbecile in front of your own mother.

CONNIE: Why not? She thinks I have polenta for brains. My father, may his soul rest in peace, you, and Rose have convinced her of that. If I won the Nobel Prize, for whatever the hell they give those damn prizes for, she'd still say I don't know how to iron and my ravioli fall apart.

JOHNNY: You're gonna give her a stroke.

CONNIE: No, I won't. She's a strong old lady.

JOHNNY: Listen, I don't like to be threatened.

CONNIE: Oh, when you need me to sign the divorce papers, you can find me at Bingo. I'm gonna be going seven nights a week.

JOHNNY: You are threatening me, aren't you?

CONNIE: You bet your sweet ass I am.

JOHNNY: *(After a moment)* Oh boy, oh boy. What a day this is gonna be. You think you've got your son's best interests at heart, but you don't. He's on the sensitive side. It's gonna hurt him all those ugly things everybody's gonna say.

CONNIE: We'll be there. We'll protect him. I'm gonna make a fresh pot of coffee, you want some?

JOHNNY: Maybe I should drink this pot first.

CONNIE: You wouldn't want to do that. You'd miss the wedding.

(JOHNNY *glares at* CONNIE *as she takes the coffee pot and disappears into the darkness. After a brief pause)*

JOHNNY: Hey, big brains, suppose tonight when the Lano boys are playing a nice slow number, the blond bombshell comes over to me and asks me to dance? What'll I do?

CONNIE: *(From the darkness. Deliberately)* You'll get up and you'll dance.

JOHNNY: *(Sneaking in a prayer, he quickly makes the sign of the cross.)* Hey, Dominic, please, I'm begging you. Twist his ankle, break his leg, do anything, but keep that bastard off the dance floor tonight!

(Blackout)

END OF PLAY

THE SHANGRI-LA MOTOR INN

CHARACTERS & SETTING

JACKIE VENTURA
FRED HENEBERRY
VINNIE VENTURA

Place: The lobby of the Shangri-La Motor Inn. A few miles outside of Utica, New York.

Time: Late evening. June 1971.

*(The lobby of the Shangri-La Motor Inn. A couple of chairs
and a small sofa surround a large and low Formica table.
The table is covered with magazines, mostly out of date,
newspapers, and a couple of ashtrays. The rest of the lobby
lies in darkness, except for the outline of the motel's sign-in
desk, which can be seen in the background. The darkness has
a pink cast to it, which comes from the light of the motel sign
spilling through an unseen window.)*

*(It is three o'clock in the morning. Lying on the sofa in a
lavender chiffon nightgown is* JACKIE VENTURA, *a woman
in her early thirties. She is rapidly saying the rosary.
Standing near her is the hotel clerk,* FRED, *an attractive
young man of the same age. He is wearing a T-shirt
and jeans. He looks slightly out of place in these clothes,
mostly because they are brand new.)*

JACKIE: *(Rapidly, almost mumbling)* Hail Mary, full of
grace, the Lord is with thee: Blessed art thou among
women; and blessed is the fruit of thy womb, Jesus....

FRED: *(Tentatively)* Excuse me...

*(*JACKIE *holds up her hand to indicate that* FRED *must wait a
second.)*

JACKIE: Holy Mary, Mother of God, pray for us sinners,
now and at the hour of our death. Amen. *(Sitting up,
slightly embarrassed)* I'm not a fanatic or anything, but
a good round on the rosary always helps clear my head.
Can I help you?

FRED: Miss...

JACKIE: *(Indicating her wedding ring)* Mrs...

FRED: Excuse me, Mrs...ah... Why don't you finish your prayers back in your room?

JACKIE: No, thank you. I'm comfortable here.

FRED: I don't think I can allow this.

JACKIE: Why not? There can't be a rule against praying in a motel lobby.

FRED: I wouldn't know about that, but it's three in the morning. My boss has rules. He says that guests hanging around this lobby, after the eleven o'clock news, make the place look like a flea bag.

JACKIE: *(Holding back a sob)* So what? *(She puts her rosary back in its case and places it on the table. She then picks up a magazine and tries to distract herself.)*

FRED: *(Very irritated)* Hey, lady...

(JACKIE suddenly bursts into tears.)

JACKIE: *(Pleading)* You're not going to send me back in that room, are you? Nobody could be that cruel.

FRED: Oh, Mrs...

(He puts his arms around JACKIE and holds her. She lets out a few huge sobs and then begins controlling herself.)

JACKIE: *(Leaving his arms)* Thank you. Thank you so very much.

FRED: Oh, I'm sorry. I hope I didn't frighten you. If I seemed too pushy, it's because I'm new at this job. In fact, this is my first night alone here.

JACKIE: Congratulations.

FRED: There's nothing for you to worry about, though. If the place happens to burst into flames, I know where all the fire extinguishers are.

JACKIE: That's good. *(She reaches for his hand.)* Thank you again.

FRED: For what?

JACKIE: You held me.

FRED: Only for a second.

JACKIE: Ah, but you're the kind of man who would have held me through the night.

FRED: I don't know about that.

JACKIE: Of course you would have. You're a giving soul. A spontaneously gentle creature.

FRED: *(Enjoying the compliment)* You're embarrassing me.

JACKIE: Be proud. You radiate warmth. Do you have any idea why? *(Fervently)* It's because you stem from a wildly compassionate people.

FRED: *(Confused)* The Irish?

JACKIE: No. The gays!

FRED: You can tell I'm gay?

JACKIE: You're not still in the attic, are you? *(Quickly, correcting herself)* Excuse me, I mean the closet.

FRED: Oh, no.

JACKIE: Good.

FRED: *(Shyly)* Would you mind telling me what tipped you off?

JACKIE: Maybe it was the tenderness in your eyes. Or the way you held me in your strong, disinterested arms. Or perhaps it was the hanky in your back pocket.

FRED: Great. It's got to be the hanky. Thanks a lot. *(He gives* JACKIE *a hug.)* Am I relieved I can be spotted right away. Last year I went to New York City for the first time. I had a hanky then. But it was white, and I carried it in my front pocket.

JACKIE: My girlfriend and I like to get to New York every other year to see a show. It's such an exciting town.

FRED: I wouldn't know. They never let me into any of the places I wanted to go. I was never dressed right. One of the bars I was desperate to get into even accused me of not being gay.

JACKIE: How terrible.

FRED: You have no idea. I saved over a year for that trip. Well, it's not going to happen again. In a couple of months I'm going to San Francisco for ten whole days. And this time, I am going to be prepared, because I heard they're even stricter there than they are in New York.

JACKIE: The best of luck.

FRED: I'm planning on having a fabulous time. I'm studying maps. Memorizing certain sections of the city, so I don't get lost. Right now, I'm an expert on the Folsom Street area.

JACKIE: How thorough.

FRED: This isn't my real occupation.

JACKIE: No?

FRED: I pump gas. But I took this extra job, because I wanted to have a few spare bucks in my pocket. You know, in case I needed to buy anything special while I was there to fit in.

JACKIE: It's always smart to have a few extra bucks taped in your bra. *(Worried he might be offended)* Excuse me, but you know what I mean.

FRED: *(Good-naturedly)* Sure.

JACKIE: *(Intently)* I'm so thrilled I found you. You wouldn't know this, but we have a lot in common. You

see, I know the gay family. I have a brother who's an
active member.

FRED: You've got a gay brother?

JACKIE: Yes, yes!

FRED: Is it possible I might know him?

JACKIE: He doesn't live in the area.

FRED: Oh. Are the two of you close?

JACKIE: We are. What a surprise he gave me yesterday.
He flew all the way from California, with his boyfriend,
to attend my wedding.

FRED: You mean, tonight's your wedding night?

JACKIE: It certainly is. That's why I'm in this dumb
chiffon thing. Usually, I like to sleep in my father's
old T-shirts.

FRED: What are you doing out here?

JACKIE: Don't ask.

FRED: Your first night of marriage. How sad. Is there
anything I can do for you?

JACKIE: *(Clutching his hand)* Keep talking to me.
(Immediately) Oh, you should have seen the commotion
those boys caused. My parents were hysterical.
My entire family and all my friends spent the day
whispering. Those guys were the center of attention at
my wedding. I'm glad nobody paid too much attention
to me, because my hair didn't come out so good. I bet if
I gave a quiz, nobody at that wedding would remember
what I wore. Maybe I was too old for bridal white.

FRED: I'm sure you looked adorable.

JACKIE: *(Ignoring him)* You know, people are smart. You
don't bring just anybody three thousand miles to your

sister's wedding and then put him at the bridal table.
People surmise.

FRED: Nobody insulted them?

JACKIE: I hope not. The Polettis, my family, usually just
say a few things behind your back. Don't get me wrong.
They don't mean any harm. But those Venturas—that's
the family I married into—I heard some of them have
mouths.... Anyway, I'm sure those boys could take care
of themselves.

FRED: Good for them.

JACKIE: Oh, you should have seen my brother's friend.
You would like him. Anybody would like him. I think
he's the most beautiful man I've ever laid eyes on.
Imagine, my puny runt of a brother, only he's not
so thin any more, I think he's lifting little weights, is,
I guess you can say, married to a...vision.

(VINNIE VENTURA *enters. He is a slightly overweight man
in his mid-thirties. He is wearing slacks and a dress shirt.*)

VINNIE: Darling, what are you doing?

JACKIE: Talking to... Excuse me, what's your name?

FRED: Fred. Fred Heneberry.

JACKIE: Fred, this is Vinnie. Vinnie Ventura. And I'm
Jackie.

VINNIE: My wife.

FRED: *(Eyeing* VINNIE *rather suspiciously, gets up and
shakes his hand)* How do you do, Mister Ventura?

VINNIE: Vinnie.

FRED: Sorry, I'm not allowed to call the guests by their
first names.

VINNIE: Who's gonna squeal? *(To* JACKIE*)* Hey, kiddo,
let's get back to the room.

JACKIE: No.

VINNIE: *(Trying to cover his embarrassment, to* FRED*)*
She's a little nervous. You know women.

JACKIE: He's gay.

VINNIE: Another one. *(Not knowing what else to say)*
How nice for you.

JACKIE: *(Intensely)* You've got to forgive me for running
out of that room. My girlfriends, God, and my father
certainly won't, so you'd better. But Vinnie, I couldn't
help myself.

VINNIE: *(Embarrassed)* Let's go back to the room and talk
about it.

JACKIE: I told you I won't go back there. We'll have our
conversation out here.

VINNIE: *(Indicating* FRED*)* Jackie...

JACKIE: He can go for a walk.

FRED: We're on a highway.

JACKIE: I noticed a diner down the road. Would you
mind getting us three coffees?

FRED: I can't leave the lobby.

JACKIE: Vinnie, give him some money.

*(*VINNIE *takes out his wallet and shoves a bill into* FRED's
hand. VINNIE *is feeling awkward and trying his best not to
act humiliated.)*

VINNIE: Here's a ten.

JACKIE: *(Generously)* You can keep the change.

FRED: I have a job I'd like to keep.

JACKIE: We'll watch the place. *(Pointing to* VINNIE*)*
He's buddies with your boss. Ralph Pastini and Vinnie
went to the Senior Ball together.

VINNIE: Well, not exactly together, Jackie. We did take girls. We double-dated.

JACKIE: *(To* FRED*)* Didn't you notice next to our reservation he wrote "no charge"? He gave us tonight as a wedding gift. We're not going to hold up the place. Vinnie, give Ralphie a call tomorrow and rave about Fred.

VINNIE: Right.

JACKIE: *(To* VINNIE*)* Give him another five for his trouble.

VINNIE: *(Takes out his wallet and shoves another bill into* FRED*'s hand)* Here you go.

FRED: *(Taking the money)* I don't know if I'm supposed to do things like this.

VINNIE: Sure you are. You're supposed to suck up to your boss's buddies. It's part of every job,

JACKIE: Make mine Sweet 'n Low with a lot of milk.

FRED: *(To* JACKIE*)* You'll be all right?

JACKIE: I'll be fine. Really.

VINNIE: I take mine black with four sugars.

FRED: Okay, but I'll be right back.

VINNIE: *(Smiling gratefully)* Thanks a lot, pal.

*(*FRED *disappears into the darkness.)*

JACKIE: I'm sorry. I'm sorry I ran out like that. Did I scare you?

VINNIE: Don't worry about it. I bet this happens all the time. *(Enticing* JACKIE*)* I have some champagne tucked away in my suitcase. I think we should open it and polish off the whole bottle. That'll loosen us up.

JACKIE: That'll give us *agita.*

VINNIE: Honey, we need to relax. No offense, but we're not spring chickens. We're not used to this wedding-night business.

JACKIE: That's not it.

VINNIE: And me! Who could believe I could be that gross. I acted like a degenerate goon. Believe me, if I had a pair of pliers here, I'd let you rip out my tongue.

JACKIE: That's not it either.

VINNIE: Hey, you've got to live your whole life with the fact that you didn't marry Bobby De Niro or Ally Pacino, right? Well, I can live with the fact that during our long life together, you'll never... *(Whispering to her)* ...touch it.

JACKIE: Vinnie, drop it!

VINNIE: It's okay. I should have never asked you to do that. At least not tonight. Not right away.

JACKIE: Believe me, that's not it.

VINNIE: You're a lady, honey.

JACKIE: Vinnie!

VINNIE: A kind of old-fashioned type...

JACKIE: For Chrissake, if you want me to touch it so bad, pull it out, right now. I'll touch it. But I'll have to touch it here. I can't go back in that room with you. You and me, we've made a mistake. We're not supposed to be married.

VINNIE: Don't say that! Give me at least twenty years before you say something awful like that.

JACKIE: All day long there were signs, but I didn't want to see them. My hair came out lousy. It rained when I entered the church. My father acted like a nut all day. And my mother, who never took a drink in her whole life, had to be carried out of my reception dead drunk by my uncles.

VINNIE: Fate didn't get your mother soused. She boozed it up because of your brother.

JACKIE: Leave my brother out of this.

VINNIE: Honey, your parents were terrified today. They didn't know what your brother and his friend were going to do. That's why your old man made such an ass of himself by insisting my old man get up and slow dance with him. He probably figured that if everybody saw the two old geezers dancing together they'd all assume it was a big joke. This way if your brother got up and twirled around with his friend everybody would think that was a joke too. Your dad wanted everybody to think that it was a crazy night for doing goofy things.

JACKIE: Let's not argue. There are so many decisions to make.

VINNIE: And we'll always make every one together.

JACKIE: Good. What are we going to do with our wedding gifts?

VINNIE: Use them.

JACKIE: That would be like stealing. People are going to know about us. Our annulment will have to be put in the paper.

VINNIE: Our what?!?

JACKIE: Could you imagine if I kept the silver tea set your Aunt Conchetta gave us? That old witch would put the evil eye on me.

VINNIE: (Pleading) We've only been married about thirteen hours. Give me another chance.

JACKIE: Did you know your Aunt Conchetta put a curse on Louise Fontana? That's why her little Rosella is bald.

VINNIE: *(Begging)* Please, let's go and talk in the room.

JACKIE: We can't go in there together. The only way we can get an annulment out of the Church is if we can honestly say we did not spend the night together. And if that sourpuss Father Polucci gives us any trouble, you know that aisle we walked down today, we'll crawl down it, like they do at Lourdes, proclaiming our innocence.

VINNIE: *(Carefully, staring at her)* Sweetheart, do you do things like this a lot?

JACKIE: What do you mean?

VINNIE: Change your mind about things suddenly? Like...ah...have you ever bought yourself a pretty dress that you were crazy about in the store, and then when you got it home, ripped it apart with your bare hands? Do you do things like that?

JACKIE: What are you driving at?

VINNIE: Sometimes bad backs run in a family. There are families that all twitch.

JACKIE: *(Defensively)* The Polettis are only the most normal, the most regular, the most average...

VINNIE: That's not the impression they gave today. And believe me, that's not the impression you're giving tonight.

JACKIE: *(Sadly)* Trust me. I know what I'm doing.

VINNIE: *(Suddenly)* Hey, I've got it! *(Lovingly)* Did you and your family feel out of your element today? Is that what's making you act peculiar? Don't worry, sweetie, you're going to eventually fit in.

JACKIE: *(Furious)* You've got to be kidding.

VINNIE: Come on, let's face it. The Venturas are a little more high-class than what you're used to.

JACKIE: They're nothing but highfalutin' show-offs. It's June, Vinnie. June. Fur coats in this heat are ridiculous. Just because your family's in the business, doesn't mean the women have to come into the reception hall looking like Italian Eskimos.

VINNIE: Jealous. You're jealous that my family made good.

JACKIE: Let's stop this. We have work to do. What are we going to tell the people at home?

VINNIE: How about this? On the honeymoon night I was such a lousy lay that even the Church is going to help you ditch me.

JACKIE: Would you calm down. You mustn't take this personally.

VINNIE: You know what your problem is? I betcha your whole life you went to sleep dreaming about this night. So, I was a disappointment. It's only because you built tonight up too much in your mind. You want a piece of advice? It's something my mother taught me. She's a wise woman. She knows life. She says, "Never, never look forward to anything. This way you'll spend your whole life disappointment free."

JACKIE: Listen to me. I'm saving our lives. You and me, we're not prepared for marriage.

VINNIE: Should we have waited until we had walkers?

JACKIE: Today, when I was standing in the reception line and everybody was handing me their envelopes, I got such a chill, because I saw our future. I smelled every meal I was going to cook for you. I heard every petty fight we were going to have. And everything was very familiar. We're destined to be a Mister and Mrs Ventura just like the last ones. We're clones.

VINNIE: No, we're not.

JACKIE: You're right. We don't have their pocketbook. You and I are much more like a Mister and Mrs Poletti.

VINNIE: We're nothing like your parents. You're not your mother. I'm not your father.

JACKIE: You're worse than my father. At least my father moved my mother down the street from his parents. You, you're moving me into your parents' converted garage. With a goddamn intercom in it.

VINNIE: Don't tell my folks, but I'll break that intercom. I'll shove my fist through it.

JACKIE: I don't want to face all those Sundays in store for us. Watching your parents or mine fight while we stuff ourselves with baked ziti.

VINNIE: *(Getting angry)* My mother's baked ziti is one of the great pleasures of my life.

JACKIE: I know that. But I don't want to be chained to those ziti every other Sunday for the rest of my life.

VINNIE: Take back what you said right now. God has big ears. Don't piss him off. Sometimes he listens to those things and punishes the people who say them. I don't want him killing my mother and taking her from me because you don't want to eat her food.

JACKIE: I take it back.

VINNIE: I can't believe this! I can't believe you want to split us up! *(Suddenly, angry)* Why the hell did you marry me?

JACKIE: I like you.

VINNIE: *(Sarcastically)* Oh yeah. Sure.

JACKIE: I may even love you. When Big Bobby got you to ask me out, I was happy. I got to know you. Like you. I was impressed with your taste in movies.

VINNIE: We have a lot in common. You were smart to accept my proposal. We both like a good game of pitch. Take a look at our record collections. They match. We're both suckers for Glen Campbell.

JACKIE: Right. And everybody around us is married. So when I said yes to you, I was thinking I could make you happy. I was thinking how proud my family was going to be at the catch I finally made. I was thinking and thinking about everything and everybody but me.

VINNIE: Here's some advice for you. Try to see the light before you say "I do" to the next jerk.

JACKIE: I wish I knew what I know now two days ago or years ago. I'm sorry, but it wasn't until after the ceremony, it wasn't until this afternoon, when I was talking to my brother....

VINNIE: Your brother!!! So all this is his fault!!!!

JACKIE: He opened my eyes. He told me incredible things.

VINNIE: Why that lousy...

JACKIE: (*Jumping up, interrupting him*) Watch it! You better watch it! You better not call him one of those ugly names.

VINNIE: (*Defending himself*) I was only gonna call him a son of a bitch. Is that permissible?

JACKIE: (*Quietly, sitting back down*) Yes.

VINNIE: That son of a bitch turned you against me. That's what tonight's about. Did he tell you you could have done better? He doesn't care that I'm a member of the Garibaldi Country Club. Oh no. He still thinks I'm low-class, right? Well, I may not be the looker that he landed, but everybody says I've got a big heart. That's got to count for something.

JACKIE: It does. Someplace I'm sure it does. But while I was talking to my brother, I finally woke up. I realized you don't marry a person. You marry into a life. And no matter what I may feel about you, you come along with the exact same life everybody else we know does. And it's one I know now I can't stand.

VINNIE: What are you planning to do? Live in orbit somewhere.

JACKIE: Do you want a marriage like Richie's?

VINNIE: Why not? He's content.

JACKIE: Then he's a dope. Did you know that Loretta tortures him when he's asleep? She told me. She pinches him and punches him in the stomach. One time she cut off some of his hair. She says she can't stop herself. And she's too embarrassed to go to a doctor. I'm worried. Some night she's going to kill him. I don't want to end up like her. *(Breaking down)* I don't want to go crazy some night and saw you apart with the electric knife my Aunt Florence gave us.

VINNIE: You're serious, aren't you?!!?

JACKIE: Yes. Vinnie, you're my only friend. You've got to forgive me, and then start helping me.

VINNIE: Helping you do what?

JACKIE: Figure out what I'm going to do with the rest of my goddamn life.

VINNIE: What about my life?

JACKIE: Don't be so selfish: You know what you want to do. You just don't have anybody to do it with. How did he do it?

VINNIE: Who?

JACKIE: My brother. How'd he end up with everything? How?! He never listened to anybody. He doesn't take my grandmother shopping every Thursday night. He wouldn't let my Dad help him choose his career like I did. God, I hate being a dental hygienist.

VINNIE: I'll let you quit. You can stay home and watch the soap operas.

JACKIE: How did he end up with the wonderful life?

VINNIE: I'm sure it's not that hot. I bet he's as miserable as everybody else.

JACKIE: Misery doesn't look that fabulous. When I saw them both, I couldn't believe my eyes. For a second I thought maybe they were kings. I didn't know if I was supposed to hug them or bow.

VINNIE: It's their suntans. They better watch it, though. In a couple of years they're going to start looking like a pair of Greek olives.

JACKIE: This afternoon my brother told me all about their married life.

VINNIE: They marry them now in California?

JACKIE: He didn't really use the word married. He calls his friend his lover. My brother has the most perfect life I ever heard about.

VINNIE: We can have a better one.

JACKIE: That is impossible. It's a good thing the other women at the wedding didn't hear about the kind of marriage those guys have. They'd kill themselves. Tomorrow they'd start flinging themselves in front of garbage trucks. You should have heard about their honeymoon.

VINNIE: How can those people have honeymoons? Don't they do it the second they lay eyes on each other?

JACKIE: They may. But my brother told me they did have a honeymoon. They drove up the coast to go to some gay resort. While they were driving, the sun was setting, and they got all excited, because they felt such a passion for each other, that they had to stop the car, run down to the beach, and make love right away. Imagine, my brother and that beautiful man, with those pretty arms, making love on the beach. Doesn't it sound like a scene from a movie?

VINNIE: *(Sarcastically)* Yeah. I think I saw it. It starred Annette Funicello and Frankie Avalon.

JACKIE: Look at what we did on the way to our honeymoon.

VINNIE: We talked. In fact we had a rather lengthy conversation.

JACKIE: Yes. About the funeral plots your Uncle Louie gave us. The great view we're going to have at Saint Agnes's Cemetery is not my idea of exciting honeymoon talk. If there were a future in store for us, we would have been in that car having serious discussions planning fun.

VINNIE: Only bums and Peter Pan get to have the fun you're thinking about. It doesn't exist in regular life. It's a lie they put on television to make us feel better. You're born, you eat, you die. That's it.

JACKIE: My brother's having fun twenty-four hours a day.

VINNIE: Then he's on drugs.

(FRED enters.)

FRED: *(Referring to the idea that JACKIE's brother is on drugs.)* Oh, I'm sorry. *(He begins passing out the coffee.)*

VINNIE: You want that kind of fun? Ask him his
pusher's name, and I'll get you whatever the hell
your brother's taking.

JACKIE: Vinnie, you're giving Fred the wrong idea.
(To FRED*)* My brother is no dope fiend. In fact, he and
his friend radiate health. Would you like to see their
picture?

FRED: You've got a photo of the hunk?

VINNIE: You've heard about him? This woman wastes
no time.

JACKIE: *(To* FRED*)* I snuck around and took a few
candids of them with my Polaroid. *(She goes to the sofa,
reaches under a cushion, and pulls out a white satin purse.)*
The wedding purse. I didn't want to leave it in the
room.

VINNIE: Of course not. I might have lost all the dough
playing solitaire.

JACKIE: *(She reaches into the purse and takes out a few
photos.)* Here he is.

FRED: Sweet Jesus!

JACKIE: Look at his plate. Only healthy stuff is on that
dish. And you should have seen the food he passed up.
His will power must be incredible.

FRED: He's beautiful.

JACKIE: *(Proudly)* I told you. That's my brother standing
behind him.

FRED: Cute.

JACKIE: *(Showing* FRED *another photo)* Here they both
are together. Look at those sparkling smiles. I'm
sure they're not smiling because they're enjoying
themselves. They're thinking about those fabulous
times they're going to be having as soon as they blow

this joint. They're thinking about the moonlight swims, cuddling in each other's arms, vacations in fancy places, going shopping, dancing till dawn with tambourines in their hands....

FRED: Boy, are they blessed.

JACKIE: What do you mean, "Are *they* blessed"? You're gay too.

FRED: Yeah, but I'm deprived. I'm a deprived gay. Lots of us are.

VINNIE: See! I knew it. *(To* JACKIE*)* You don't know anything real about his people.

JACKIE: I certainly do.

VINNIE: You don't know gay people. All you know is your brother.

JACKIE: I read a book.

VINNIE: Books lie. *(To* FRED*)* Fred, do me a favor, can you please tell her some things about your life.

FRED: Look, I'm a kind of private person.

VINNIE: *(Taking out his wallet)* Here's a twenty. Just give us a few facts.

FRED: All you want are some facts? *(He takes the money.)*

JACKIE: Forget facts. They're not important. Tell us what you're supposed to do.

FRED: What do you mean?

JACKIE: Like Vinnie here. For the rest of his life he's supposed to work five and a half days a week in his father's fur shop. He's supposed to get two weeks off every August when he'll take his wife, and the two kids he's supposed to have, up to a camp in the Adirondacks. In a couple of years he's supposed to start drinking too much. At forty-five he's supposed to have his first and only affair. It'll be brief. His wife will find out about it and make the rest of his life miserable. He's supposed to get his first heart attack in his late fifties and die maybe ten years later. These last ten years are supposed to be lousy because he'll be watching his weight all the time and won't be able to eat or drink anything he really wants.

Now, me. I'm supposed to devote my life to a man like that. I'm supposed to have his children. I'm not supposed to have a career, but I'll get a job that'll bring some extra dollars into the house. This way we'll be able to act like big shots and buy our kids their first cars when they go off to their schools. I'm supposed to dye my hair the second I start going gray. I'm supposed to cut coupons out of every newspaper and magazine I can get my hands on in order to save ten cents. I'm supposed to learn a hobby, like crocheting or ceramics or knitting scarves. I'll probably get addicted to my hobby. This will give everyone a good reason to laugh at me. I'm supposed to develop insomnia which I'll cure all by myself by either taking pills or sneaking a few late-night drinks. In time I'm supposed to bury my husband, get severely depressed, either die or take in a boarder. Now, what are you supposed to do?

FRED: Nothing like that I hope.

JACKIE: *(Breaking down)* You see. They have the best lives.

FRED: Wait a minute. I work very hard.

VINNIE: Life's a bitch, isn't it? It's rough. It's work, work, work. It's a grind, right?

JACKIE: *(To FRED)* What do you do on Saturday nights?

FRED: I'm working.

JACKIE: *(Quickly)* What did you do before you got this job?

FRED: Worked at the gas station. That was before they cut my hours. I've got to tell you, I'm desperate to get into something cleaner, like maybe even motel management or selling jewelry. My friends think I'm crazy. They say it's much hotter being a grease monkey. But then they don't have to go around smelling like the inside of an engine twenty-four hours a day.

JACKIE: How do you spend your Sunday afternoons?

FRED: Lately, cleaning these damned nails. They're filthy constantly. There is simply nothing you can do about them.

VINNIE: You see, your brother's a liar. In this life nobody has it any better than anyone else. Maybe they did do it once on a beach. So what? Jackie, if that's all you want, we'll forget about going to Washington, DC, and I'll drive you straight to Coney Island.

FRED: Gee, I never did it on a beach.

VINNIE: *(Jumping up and hugging* FRED*)* God bless you. *(To* JACKIE*)* Did you hear him, honey? He never did it outside.

FRED: I didn't say that Mister Ventura. I've had some of the hottest times of my life in the great outdoors. Once I was seeing this forest ranger...

JACKIE: *(To* VINNIE*)* Aren't they adventurous?

FRED: ...and I used to meet him near the lookout tower....

JACKIE: *(Romantically)* Were you desperately in love?

FRED: He was great, great sex, and a sweet, sweet man, but a bit vapid. You could never get him to take that damn uniform off. And during sex he liked to be called Smokey.

VINNIE: Sex, why that may be it! Jackie, it's all clear now. I can see what's wrong. You're getting sex mixed up with love and love mixed up with life, and it's

making your brain like pasta *fazula*. You see, God is fair.
He always strives for balance. That's why he makes
homely people smart, beautiful people dumb. He gives
all the power to men, but he makes women live longer.
Balance, Jackie. All balance. Because most of our people
are peasants, he makes us jolly and good cooks. He
loves to sprinkle our pathetic lives with tiny treats.
Now, the gays. Their lives can be tough. There's always
somebody hating them. That's why God gives them
great sex. It's their tidbit. I wonder what he does for
the Blacks and the Polish people.

FRED: You can't possibly believe that drivel that's
pouring out of your mouth.

JACKIE: How humiliating. *(To* VINNIE*)* And you were
lucky enough to go to two years of business school.
What did you do? Leave your brains at Dunkin' Donuts
every morning?

VINNIE: Your brother filled your head with nonsense
today. The Lord wants to give you a quiet life. Be
grateful. We're getting the better deal. All he's giving
your brother are a few wild times. That's crumbs.
Crumbs from the table.

JACKIE: You're talking like a dimwit. Fred, to set the
record straight, we have great sex too.

VINNIE: Jackie! Please! Be quiet.

JACKIE: I'm sure Fred didn't think I made it to this age
without a teensy bit of a past.

VINNIE: *(To* FRED*)* I know all about it. It happened
before we met. She only did it once, and it was with
a complete stranger.

JACKIE: I met him in the Hotel Utica when I had to
deliver poor old Miss Higgins her dentures. She's
bedridden, and she lives there.

VINNIE: Fred's not interested in this.

FRED: Yes, I am. I love hearing about first times.

JACKIE: Well, I got so depressed seeing that old lady all alone that when I finished visiting her I headed straight for the bar and ordered myself a drink. A Boci Ball.
I had them send one up to Miss Higgins too. And there he was ordering himself a martini. He looked at me.
I looked at him....

VINNIE: *(To* JACKIE*)* You could have been killed. Some of those guys have stilettos taped to their ankles.

JACKIE: *(To* VINNIE*)* He was a pussycat. *(To* FRED*)* I was with him six and a half hours and a more patient man you never want to meet. It was my first time, and I was scared so it was hurting. So we'd stop and watch some television, and then we'd try again and stop and watch some more. Thank God *Spartacus* was on.

FRED: How sensible.

JACKIE: It was. And once I relaxed, it was quite nice.

FRED: My first experience was nice too. Only I was twelve, and I didn't have six and a half hours. Tommy and I had ten minutes. That's how long it took his mother to go pick up his father. *(To* VINNIE*)* How about you?

VINNIE: I don't feel like talking about it.

JACKIE: Come on. It's just us here.

VINNIE: This is exactly what I had in mind for tonight. Sitting around swapping dirty stories.

JACKIE: *(To* FRED, *understandingly)* I guess he's shy about these matters.

VINNIE: *(Awkwardly)* I'm not shy. After high school, I went into a slump. I was jittery all the time. So my Uncle Frankie took me to a lady of the evening.

(Whispering to FRED*)* A whore. She had the reputation of being very exotic. *(Whispering again to* FRED*)* The guys said she would do anything for a buck. She had this orange, orange hair. She called herself Tangerine. Very exotic. Well, my uncle told her to give me the works.

JACKIE: Where did he think he was sending you? To the beauty parlor?

VINNIE: She did give me the works. And I was not that impressed.

JACKIE: That's too bad. The poor thing was probably having a bad day.

FRED: Or life.

JACKIE: True. You know, what I did in that hotel room was a mortal sin. I thought that was the reason I had such a fabulous time. Today, I found out that married couples should be that daring. You may be right, Vinnie. This is all my brother's fault. He should have come home at Christmas and talked to me. *(Staring at the photo in her hand)* Two Prince Charmings that found each other.

FRED: *(Looking over* JACKIE's *shoulder at the photo)* I hope they're good to each other. I wonder if sometimes he brings your brother little treats.

JACKIE: My brother should thank the Lord if this one comes home every night. He should get down on his knees.

FRED: I'm sure he does.

JACKIE: I don't think so. My brother's not religious.

VINNIE: Jesus Christ!!! Am I blind! You can't stand my guts, can you?

JACKIE: Oh no! No!

VINNIE: I disgust you, don't I? Revolt you. The thought of me makes you nauseous, right?

JACKIE: No! You're not evil like me. You're sensitive, warm....

VINNIE: *(Grabbing the photo out of* FRED's *hand)* But I'm not like Mister Hot Shit, am I?

JACKIE: *(Reaching for the picture)* Be careful.

VINNIE: Of course. *(Handing the picture back to* JACKIE. *To* FRED) She's going to be keeping her brother and Tarzan under her pillow. You know, Jackie, there are plenty of women who would crawl the length of a bowling alley to be with me. Yes, siree. Plenty. And men too. Yeah. Once, when I was in the train station, two very attractive guys gave me the eye.

JACKIE: I'm glad, Vinnie.

VINNIE: I bet if I were of Fred's persuasion, he might be interested in being a Mister Fred Heneberry Ventura. Right pal?

FRED: Well...ah...

VINNIE: Right?

FRED: I hardly know you.

VINNIE: But you find me attractive, don't you?

FRED: You're a friendly looking guy.

VINNIE: Don't be embarrassed, but I turn you on, right?

FRED: How can I answer anything like that?

VINNIE: Easy. You say yes or no. What is it?

JACKIE: Where are your manners?

VINNIE: I sent them back to my Mom. She can have them bronzed and keep them next to my baby shoes. *(To* FRED) Well?

FRED: *(Quietly)* No.

VINNIE: Why?

FRED: I'm sorry, Mister Ventura, you just don't turn me on.

VINNIE: But why?

FRED: It's so subjective.

VINNIE: Of course it is. Come on. I'm not going to let you off the hook.

FRED: Well... There's no mystery about you.

VINNIE: No mystery, huh? How about that. No mystery. Maybe I should get a mask. Jackie, if I looked like the Lone Ranger, would you hop in the sack with me?

JACKIE: All Fred is saying is that you're the kind of guy who wears his heart on his sleeve. The second you walk into a room everybody knows what you're thinking.

FRED: *(Defending himself)* That's what I meant.

VINNIE: What have I got in my head, a hole or a bay window?

JACKIE: No. You have an outgoing personality. You're generous. Even with your laughs. Everybody says that about you. You love giving people a good time. Even if it means making fun of yourself, describing some of the stupid things you do. You're like a young Paulie Telephano. Now, there was a man.

VINNIE: He was a *citrullo.*

JACKIE: No, he wasn't. He was loved by everybody. Remember his funeral? How crowded it was, and how we all laughed telling old Paulie stories.

VINNIE: At my funeral I'd appreciate it if everybody would cry.

FRED: What's a *citrullo?*

VINNIE: No wonder you're running away from me. You don't want to be saddled to one. You don't want to be a Mrs *Citrullo*.

FRED: Excuse me, but what is a *citrullo*?

VINNIE: He's a doormat, a turkey, a softie, a moosh-a-moosh. He's me. A dufus, with a heart of gold, who smells of his mama's tomato sauce.

JACKIE: Don't torture yourself. You're not one.

VINNIE: *(Getting hysterical)* I'm one!

JACKIE: No!!! Get me a Bible. I'll swear on it.

VINNIE: Oh God, I know I'm one.

FRED: You may have dufus tendencies, Everybody does. But you're not a true one. You don't even dress like one.

VINNIE: Do they have a fashion magazine?

FRED: You know what I'm talking about. Those guys who never grew out of wearing those hats with earlappers.

VINNIE: Should I go get mine? It's in my glove compartment.

JACKIE: You only wear it in the winter.

VINNIE: *(To* JACKIE*)* I'm a dufus, not a moron.

JACKIE: Fred, help me. Say something to him.

FRED: Mister Ventura, I didn't mean to hurt your feelings. I didn't. Honestly.

VINNIE: That's life.

(FRED *sheepishly disappears into the darkness and sits behind the desk.)*

VINNIE: I've got to lie down. *(He goes over to the couch and sprawls out on it.)* Be yourself. What a crock. Nobody wants you to be yourself. Everybody wants you to be somebody else. The true good guys, nobody cares for them.

FRED: *(From the darkness)* That's certainly true.

JACKIE: *(Shouting into the darkness)* No, it's not!

VINNIE: *(Shouting into the darkness)* How do you know?

FRED: *(Coming from behind his desk and out of the darkness)* You are looking at a double-dufus. To my gay friends I'm a shit-kicking farmer dufus who's a cultural retard. And to my straight chums I'm known as the dingdong who always seems to get stepped on. Move over.

(FRED joins VINNIE on the couch. VINNIE lies one way, and FRED lies the other way.)

VINNIE: You know, I'm beginning to feel better. There's something relaxing about coming out...

FRED: There certainly is.

VINNIE: ...and saying it loud and clear. I'm a *citrullo.*

FRED: Me too. But I'm working on it.

JACKIE: Would you guys stop this.

VINNIE: You know, Fred, I love animals. I love them. And I'm in the fur business. Now, who would sell fur coats all day long and then walk out of his old man's store and sign a petition to prevent cruelty to animals?

FRED: A dork. And who would fall hopelessly in love with a handsome slob one week, and by the next week become, not his lover, not his new hot affair, but his cheerful little mop?

VINNIE: A moosh-a-moosh.

FRED: Do you know what the bastard called me? Freddie Fantastik.

VINNIE: But you're not like that now.

FRED: I'm trying like hell to break out of dufydom. The trouble with dufuses is they all think they're great guys. But they're not. They spend their whole lives always looking for a bigger ass to kiss.

JACKIE: You men. You always think you've got it rougher than everybody else. Just try being a lady *citrullo.*

VINNIE: But you're not one.

JACKIE: Is that why, while I was dating Sal, every time he took me to the restaurant he seated me behind a huge potted plant?

VINNIE: He probably was looking for a place he could be alone with you. The poor thing still lives with his Aunt Theresa.

JACKIE: Oooh, maybe you're right. Every once and a while he did try to sneak in a feel. And I'd have to stab him with my fork.

VINNIE: I told you.

JACKIE: But when I was twelve, I bought a carved box for my love letters. Vinnie, it's still empty.

VINNIE: You know why the guys left you alone? They were afraid of you. Word was out that you had very high standards.

JACKIE: I don't believe you.

VINNIE: All the guys think of you as elegant.

JACKIE: No!

VINNIE: Yeah.

JACKIE: *(Proudly)* Really?

VINNIE: Yeah. They call you a classy lady with great skin.

JACKIE: Why didn't anybody ever tell me? Why didn't anybody tell me I was thought of as... What else did they say I was?

VINNIE: Statuesque.

JACKIE: Statuesque. How about that. Why didn't anybody tell me?

VINNIE: I did. But who would believe Bozo.

JACKIE: You should have convinced me.

VINNIE: Fred, my whole life, whatever I say rolls off everybody's back. When am I going to be believed?

FRED: As soon as you change.

VINNIE: At my age? How? What can I do?

FRED: Start doing unexpected things. Shock yourself, and then start shocking other people.

VINNIE: Okay. *(He gets up from the couch and begins pacing around the room.)* I'm leaving the fur business.

FRED: Bravo! *(He sits up.)*

JACKIE: I was somebody else all these years, and I never knew it. If I knew I was so sophisticated, I wouldn't have become a dental hygienist. I would have gone to beauty school instead. By now, I would have had my own business. I could have called my shop Rapunzel's.

VINNIE: I'm not going back to Utica yet. *(To* JACKIE*)* And I'm not going to Washington, DC, like we planned. I'm heading all by myself to Niagara Falls. *(To* FRED*)* Jackie didn't want to go there because it sounded too old-fashioned. Someplace our parents would go. But I think it would be incredible seeing tons and tons of water with colored lights on it. Betcha it's better than Disneyland. *(To both* JACKIE *and* FRED*)* I'll stay in Niagara Falls as long as the water holds my interest, and then from there, who knows where I'll land.

FRED: That sounds great. Leaving everything. Getting in the car. Hitting the road. It's so Fifties. So Kerouac.

VINNIE: What can I say? I'm behind the times. But I'll catch up.

JACKIE: You've got to come home with me. We owe a lot of people an explanation, and we've got to think of a good one. One that will make people still like us.

VINNIE: I've never been anywhere. This could be exciting. Who knows if I'll ever get back.

JACKIE: You're talking stupid. You need your friends, your cousins. You need a crowd around you twenty-four hours a day.

VINNIE: I may be lonely, but so what. I'm going to be busy making myself interesting. (*To* FRED) Where's the Grand Canyon? I want to go there.

FRED: It's in Arizona, and I hear it's terrific. They have these mules you have to take if you want to go down.

JACKIE: What do you know about sitting on an animal? You'll fall off and break your neck.

VINNIE: I'll take mule-riding lessons.

JACKIE: How are you going to support yourself?

VINNIE: When I run out of my half of the honeymoon money, I'll do what everybody else does. I'll go to work.

JACKIE: You mean this, don't you? You're going to take off. Just like my brother.

VINNIE: Does anybody know how long it would take to get from the Buffalo area to Vegas?

FRED: Two, maybe three days.

JACKIE: The men are busy planning breathtaking things while the woman is sent home to do all the dirty work. (*To* FRED) I expected more sensitivity from you.

FRED: Sorry.

VINNIE: Don't feel sorry for her. With her half of the honeymoon money she can go wherever she wants.

JACKIE: How will I get there? Walk?

VINNIE: Take a bus,

JACKIE: Buses make me carsick.

FRED: *(To* JACKIE*)* Then why don't you go with him.

(JACKIE *looks anxiously at* VINNIE.*)*

VINNIE: *(After a moment)* No!

JACKIE: He doesn't want his style cramped.

FRED: It won't be. Why don't you travel like buddies? You'll keep each other company in the car. When you get to a town, if you want, you can split up.

VINNIE: I don't want anybody near me who ever pitied me.

JACKIE: I never pitied you. Never. I care for you. I pitied us. I pitied the life we were supposed to have. The one you're ditching.

VINNIE: When I finally come back to the old hometown, people are going to be amazed. They're going to want to buy me drinks, sit next to me in restaurants, listen to my stories, take my advice.

JACKIE: I doubt it.

VINNIE: You'll see.

JACKIE: No way. It'll never happen.

VINNIE: When you see what I've turned myself into, you're going to take your pretty fists and beat your pillow every night.

JACKIE: That may be true. I may see how exciting you've become and get very depressed. But to everybody else you'll be the same old Vinnie.

VINNIE: Oh my God, I hope not.

FRED: That's not true. People will see the change.

JACKIE: If I go home alone, the story of our honeymoon night will become a classic. It doesn't matter what I tell people. They'll think that Vinnie acted like such a goof on his honeymoon night that he couldn't come home for ten, twenty years.

VINNIE: I know these people. She's right. When I die, instead of a funeral, they're going to give me a roast.

FRED: Stop talking like that.

JACKIE: This is all my fault. I'm going to have to act like a big girl and make a sacrifice. Vinnie, I'm coming with you.

VINNIE: Why?

JACKIE: You need me. I've got to help you change your image. I owe that to you. I'm going to start a program of sending letters home. Like, "Vinnie's working construction here in New Orleans." I've always wanted to see the French Quarter. Or, "Here we are in the Rockies. Vinnie's working and studying to be a veterinarian, and I'm in beauty school." Letters and postcards like that.

VINNIE: Why would you want to go roaming around the country with a dufus?

JACKIE: I wouldn't. I want to go searching for a home with an adventurer, a pioneer.

VINNIE: I can't do what Fred suggested. I love you. I can't travel around just being your buddy.

JACKIE: Vinnie, Fred meant something like my brother and his friend. You know, gay buddies.

FRED: That's right. Partners, who aren't afraid of showing affection....

JACKIE: *(Interrupting* FRED*)* Tons of it.

FRED: And...

JACKIE: We know what that "and" is, don't we, honey? *(She stares lovingly at* VINNIE.*)*

VINNIE: *(Hesitantly)* Do you think we can pull it off?

JACKIE: I'd like to try, love. Please let's try.

*(*VINNIE *stares back at* JACKIE, *lovingly.)*

FRED: Hey, folks, I've got work to do.

JACKIE: And we have plans to make.

VINNIE: *(To* FRED*)* Look, I'm going to drop you a note. If we all happen to be out West at the same time, we'll get together.

FRED: Wouldn't that be special.

JACKIE: Listen to my vagabond.

*(*VINNIE *goes over to* FRED *and gives him a hug.)*

VINNIE: Watch out for yourself, pal. *(To* JACKIE*)* Come on...buddy.

*(*JACKIE *picks up her rosary case from the table and heads for the door.)*

JACKIE: *(Blowing* FRED *a kiss)* See you.

FRED: Fun dreams.

*(*JACKIE *and* VINNIE *exit.* FRED *smiles and stares at the door a moment.)*

JACKIE: *(From outside)* Sweetheart, go and open the champagne. I'll be right there. *(She comes back into the lobby.)* Forgot my purse.

FRED: *(Getting it for her)* Oh. Here.

JACKIE: Next Thursday, I don't know where I'll be or what I'll be doing. That's the first time in my entire life I can ever say anything that beautiful. I'm so happy.

(She hugs FRED and begins to exit.)

(Fade out)

END OF PLAY